DAY HIKES IN
YOSEMITE
NATIONAL PARK

25 FAVORITE HIKES

by Robert Stone

Photographs by Robert Stone
Published by:
Day Hike Books, Inc.
114 South Hauser Box 865
Red Lodge, MT 59068
Layout & Design: Paula Doherty
Copyright 1997
Library of Congress Catalog Card Number: 96-96977

Distributed by:
ICS Books, Inc.
1370 E. 86th Place
Merrillville, IN 46410
1-800-541-7323
Fax 1-800-336-8334

TABLE OF CONTENTS

THE HIKES

In the Valley

Glacier Point Road

The Giant Sequoias

North Yosemite—Tioga Road

About the Hikes and Yosemite National Park

Yosemite National Park lies in central California on the western slope of the Sierra Nevada. The park's dramatic topography, sculpted by ancient glaciers, encompasses 1,189 square miles (760,917 acres). The elevations range from 2,000 feet in the west to 13,000 feet in the east. Although the park has 196 miles of roads, more than 90 percent of Yosemite is roadless wilderness with more than 750 miles of trails.

Yosemite Valley and Mariposa Grove were designated a state park in 1864 by Abraham Lincoln. In 1890, Yosemite was established as America's third national park. It is among the world's best known and one of the most visited national treasures, with more than four million annual visitors.

Yosemite National Park's crown jewel is Yosemite Valley, a picturesque, seven-mile gorge chiseled by giant glaciers and carved by the Merced River. The Merced River, flowing through the heart of this three-quarter-mile wide valley floor, is surrounded by lush meadows and pristine pine and fir tree groves. The valley is home to 3,000-foot walls of granite massifs, smooth domes, and an abundance of spectacular waterfalls leaping over steep cliffs from the hanging valleys above. Among the granite monoliths within the valley are Half Dome, Clouds Rest, Royal Arches, Cathedral Rock, Three Brothers, and the largest granite rock on earth, El Capitan, rising 3,593 feet (over a half mile) above the valley. The numerous waterfalls include Nevada Fall (594 feet), Illilouette Fall (370 feet), Staircase Falls (1,300 feet), Bridalveil Fall (620 feet), Ribbon Fall (1,612 feet), Vernal Fall (317 feet), Sentinel Fall (2,000 feet), and Yosemite Falls (2,425 feet), which is the highest falls in North America and fifth highest in the world. Nevada Fall and Vernal Fall stair-step the Merced River into Yosemite Valley, dropping 2,000 feet in 1.5 miles. The peak flow of these dramatic waterfalls is in the spring when the majority of snowfall melts.

Beyond the valley is Tuolumne Meadows and the Tioga Pass. Tioga Road/Highway 120 West is the route to Tuolumne Meadows. This route was originally a mining road that was first completed in 1883, known as the Great Sierra Wagon Road. The Tioga Road was upgraded in 1961 and is now the highest paved auto route in California, crossing Tioga Pass at 9,945 feet.

The Tuolumne region was formed by an enormous glacier measuring 60 miles long and 2,000 feet thick. It carved out the largest subalpine meadow in the Sierra Nevada, Tuolumne Meadows, measuring 2.5 miles long by a half mile wide. Tuolumne Meadows stands at an elevation of 8,600 feet. It is surrounded by exposed granite domes, polished smooth by the scouring ice; serrated, snow-capped mountain peaks; alpine lakes; deep canyons; and the Tuolumne River, which carves a winding path through this northern terrain. A variety of trails begin at the meadows, from day hikes to extended backcountry trips. Some trails lead over granite ridges from one mountain lake to another. Others lead through canyons along rivers and streams, including the John Muir Trail to Mount Whitney. The elevations for the hikes in this area range from 7,000 feet to 13,000 feet.

Yosemite is also home to three giant sequoia groves—Mariposa Grove, Tuolumne Grove, and Merced Grove. Giant sequoias are among the oldest and largest of all living things, dating back as far as 3,000 years. These massive trees grow as tall as 320 feet and as wide as 35 feet in diameter. They are resistant to disease, insects, and fire. The largest and most visited of these groves is the Mariposa Grove, boasting more than 500 ancient sequoias in a 250-acre area.

There are four major access roads into Yosemite National Park. From the south, out of Fresno, is Highway 41, entering the park near Wawona. From the west is Highway 140, out of Merced, entering at El Portal/Arch Rock. From the north is Highway 120 East from Groveland, entering at Big Oak Flat.

From the east, open only during the summer, is Highway 120 West from Lee Vining, entering the park near Tuolumne Meadows.

The Day Hikes guide to Yosemite National Park focuses on 25 favorite day hikes of various lengths inside the park's border. The hikes have been chosen for their outstanding beauty and variety. Most of these hikes require easy to moderate effort, unless otherwise noted, and are timed at a leisurely rate. Each hike has its own description, driving, and hiking directions, plus an adjoining map. The trails are detailed on the United States Geological Survey 7.5 series topographical maps, which are listed with each hike. They are also detailed on the Trails Illustrated Map (Yosemite National Park #206) and a various assortment of other trail maps. These maps can be purchased at most Yosemite stores and area sporting good stores.

To learn more about this incredible national park, visit any of Yosemite's four visitor centers. They offer current information on hiking trails, interpretive programs, animals, geological and historical exhibits, books, films, and maps.

As for attire and equipment, hiking shoes offer the best support and are preferable for all of these hikes. A rain poncho, sunscreen, mosquito repellent, and drinking water are recommended. Pack a lunch and enjoy a picnic at scenic outlooks, rivers, streams, or wherever you find the best spot.

Enjoy your hike!

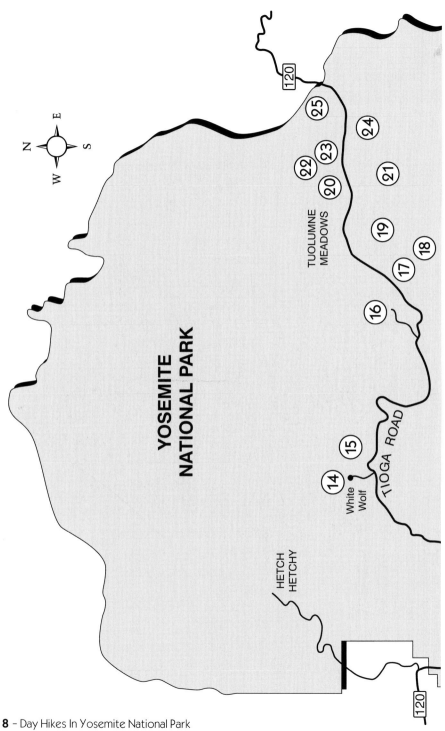

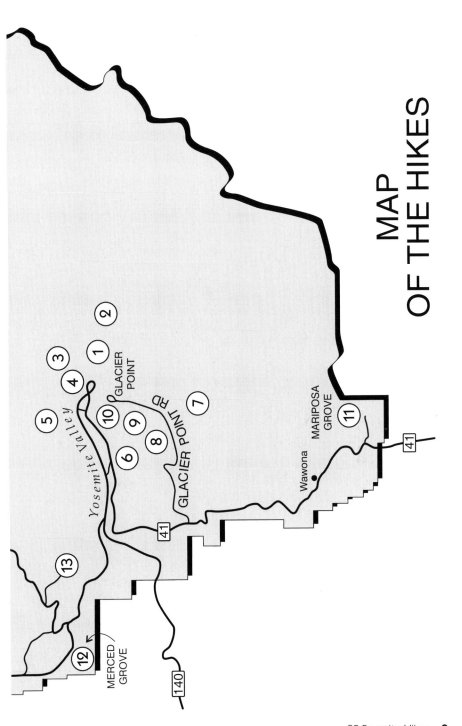

MAP
OF THE HIKES

Hikes 1 & 2
Vernal Fall and Nevada Fall

Summary of the hikes: These first two hikes head up the Merced River Canyon between Half Dome and Glacier Point among sheer granite walls and deep gorges. The trail parallels the Merced River to the base and to the top of both Vernal Fall and Nevada Fall. These falls are part of Merced Canyon's "Giant Staircase." This glacial stairway plunges 317 feet at Vernal Fall and 594 feet at Nevada Fall. The trail to the falls contains stunning views of these two world-class waterfalls, plus views of Glacier Point, Half Dome, Illilouette Fall, and Upper Yosemite Fall. The hikes cross the Merced River four times via bridges. Along the Mist Trail, mist from the large volume of water plunging over Vernal Fall sprays the canyon walls that are carpeted with moss and ferns (photo on page 26). Early in the season, the mist also sprays the trail and hikers alike. Rain gear is recommended, or you will get soaked.

The trailhead for both hikes is the beginning of the John Muir Trail. The John Muir Trail leads south to the summit of Mount Whitney, 212 miles away.

Caution: Do not swim in the pools above either waterfall. They may look safe and inviting, but they do contain strong currents. The consequences of going in could effect the rest of your vacation.

Driving directions for hikes 1 & 2: From Yosemite Valley, take the free shuttle bus to the Happy Isles Nature Center/ Stop No. 16 at the east end of the valley.

From Curry Village, walk one mile southeast along the footpath parallel to the shuttle bus road to the Happy Isles Nature Center.

A map is on page 13.

Hike 1
Vernal Fall

Hiking distance: 3 miles round trip
Hiking time: 2.5 hours
Elevation gain: 1,000 feet
Topo: U.S.G.S. Half Dome

Hiking directions: From the Happy Isles Nature Center, cross the bridge over the Merced River. The trail begins on a wide, paved path curving up canyon past enormous boulders. The Merced River rages downstream on your right. Across the canyon in a narrow gorge, Illilouette Fall plunges 370 feet over a vertical cliff. At 0.8 miles, the Vernal Fall Bridge crosses the Merced River. From this bridge is a dramatic view up river of Vernal Fall, along with Mount Broderick and the bell-shaped Liberty Cap looming above. For many, this is an excellent turnaround spot for a 1.6 mile round-trip hike.

To reach the top of Vernal Fall, continue uphill on the south side of the Merced River. A quarter mile past the bridge is a fork in the trail. Bear left, towards Vernal Fall, along the canyon edge on the Mist Trail (photo on page 26). (The right fork is the John Muir Trail, a horse route leading to the top of Nevada Fall and the return loop of Hike 2.) The Mist Trail is a steep series of granite steps. During this portion of the trail, you will feel the mist and see the rainbows from the powerful, 100-foot wide falls. Use caution, as the steps can be wet and slippery. At the top of Vernal Fall, large granite slabs and a pipe railing lead down to the brink. Then, follow the river upstream a short distance to Silver Apron, a 200-foot cascade sliding over smooth rocks into the green water of Emerald Pool. This is an excellent area to relax and enjoy some time as a reward for the climb. Swimming in Emerald Pool is not recommended, as it could be very uncomfortable going over Vernal Fall.

If you wish to hike to the top of Nevada Fall, continue with the next hike. If not, return along the same trail. An alternative trail is to return via Clark Point, following a half-mile trail up a series of switchbacks to the John Muir Trail. At Clark Point, proceed to the right, heading back to the Mist Trail. Cross the Vernal Fall Bridge and return to the nature center.

Hike 2
Nevada Fall

Hiking distance: 6 miles round trip (total of Hikes 1 & 2)
Hiking time: 5 hours
Elevation gain: 1,900 feet
Topo: U.S.G.S. Half Dome

Hiking directions: From the top of Vernal Fall and Silver Apron, where Hike 1 left off, hike upstream to a bridge, and cross the Merced River to the north side of the canyon. The trail to the top of Nevada Fall at the head of the canyon gains 900 feet in 0.9 miles via switchbacks and granite steps. Near the top, the trail curves along the base of Liberty Cap to a junction. The right fork leads down to the falls. (The left fork leads to Little Yosemite Valley and Half Dome.) At Nevada Fall, just before the bridge, a side trail leads to a spectacular lookout at the brink of the falls. To return, you may follow the same trail back or make a loop via the John Muir Trail.

To return along the John Muir Trail, cross the bridge over the Merced River above Nevada Fall to the south canyon wall. Within minutes is a trail junction. Stay to the right, continuing along the John Muir Trail. (The left fork, Panorama Trail, leads to Glacier Point.) From this side of the canyon are magnificent views of Liberty Cap towering above Nevada Fall (cover photo). Continue downhill one mile to another trail junction at Clark Point. Take the left trail downhill 0.4 miles, and rejoin the Mist Trail. Take the trail to the left, crossing the Vernal Fall Bridge, and finish the remaining 0.8 miles to the nature center.

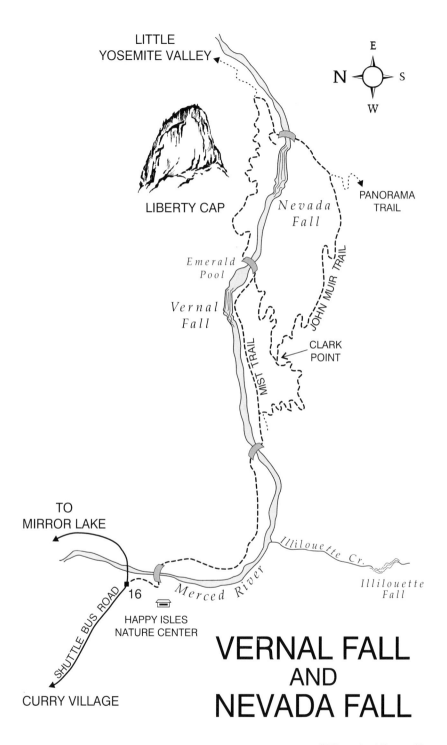

LITTLE
YOSEMITE VALLEY

LIBERTY CAP

Nevada Fall

PANORAMA
TRAIL

Emerald Pool

Vernal Fall

JOHN MUIR TRAIL

CLARK
POINT

MIST TRAIL

TO
MIRROR LAKE

Illilouette Cr.

Illilouette Fall

Merced River

16

HAPPY ISLES
NATURE CENTER

SHUTTLE BUS ROAD

CURRY VILLAGE

VERNAL FALL
AND
NEVADA FALL

Hike 3
Mirror Lake and Tenaya Canyon Loop

Hiking distance: 4.4 mile loop
Hiking time: 2 hours
Elevation gain: 200 feet
Topo: U.S.G.S. Half Dome and Yosemite Falls

Summary of hike: This hike follows Tenaya Creek up the glaciated Tenaya Canyon. The trail travels through a cedar, fir, and oak tree forest. The hike includes a visit to what was once Mirror Lake. The lake has filled in and become a marshy area with a shallow pool of water and a sand bar beach. From the lake is a magnificent view of Mount Watkins and one of Yosemite's premiere views of Half Dome.

Driving directions: Automobiles are no longer allowed in this portion of the valley. From Yosemite Valley, take the shuttle bus to Mirror Lake/Stop No. 17, or walk to the trailhead a quarter mile east of the stables at the end of the valley.

Hiking directions: The trailhead begins at the Tenaya Bridge. Before crossing the stone bridge, take the footpath to the right and a quick left, heading upstream along the south bank of Tenaya Creek. The trail gently climbs past massive, moss-covered boulders to the east shore of Mirror Lake. Continue up canyon 2.1 miles to a bridge. From the bridge, the trail loops back along the northwest side of the creek. 0.3 miles from the bridge is the Snow Creek Trail leading to Tuolumne Meadows. Continue down canyon. Upon reaching the Mirror Lake meadow, there is an awesome view of Half Dome. Mirror Lake used to carry its reflection. From here you may take either the foot-path to the right of the asphalt road, or follow the pedestrian-only road. Both will lead back to the trailhead.

Note: This trail is also used by horses, which adds an extra fragrance and a human-friendly assortment of flies.

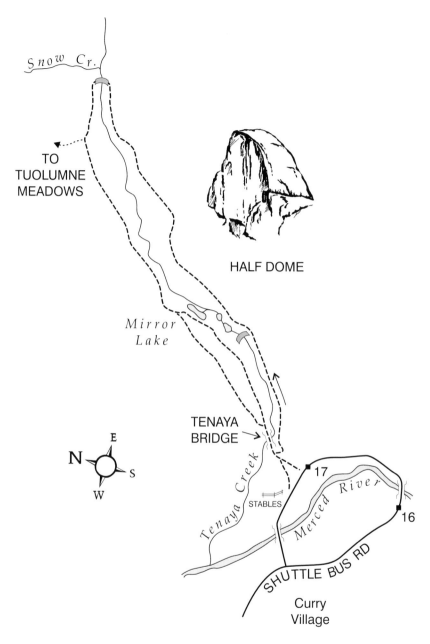

Snow Cr.

TO
TUOLUMNE
MEADOWS

HALF DOME

Mirror
Lake

TENAYA
BRIDGE

N
E
S
W

STABLES

17

Merced River

16

Tenaya Creek

SHUTTLE BUS RD

Curry
Village

MIRROR LAKE
AND TENAYA CANYON

Hike 4
East Valley Loop along the Merced River

Hiking distance: 2.5 mile loop
Hiking time: 1.5 hours
Elevation gain: Level
Topo: U.S.G.S. Half Dome

Summary of hike: This valley loop trail is an easy stroll following the banks of the Merced River at the east end of the valley. The hike includes a visit to the Happy Isles Nature Center and the tumbling whitewater of the Merced River at Happy Isles. The trail starts near Curry Village.

Driving directions: Park in the Curry Village parking lot or take the Yosemite Valley shuttle bus to Stop No. 14 or No. 15. The trail is to the south of the shuttle bus road.

Hiking directions: From the southeast corner of the Curry Village parking lot, take the footpath parallel to the shuttle bus road. Head east towards Happy Isles, passing the employee cabins on your right. Continue one mile to Happy Isles. Turn right towards the nature center, and cross the bridge over the Merced River. This is a good opportunity to enjoy the Happy Isles area and the nature center. To continue with the hike, take the trail to the left (north), heading downstream along the east bank of the river. (The trail to the right leads to Vernal and Nevada Falls, Hikes 1 and 2.) Continue along the river one mile to the horse stables. Cross Clarks Bridge over the Merced River. The footpath soon passes the entrances to Upper and Lower Pines Campgrounds. Turn right at the shuttle bus road, heading towards Stoneman Meadow. This leads to the Curry Village parking lot on the left and completes the loop.

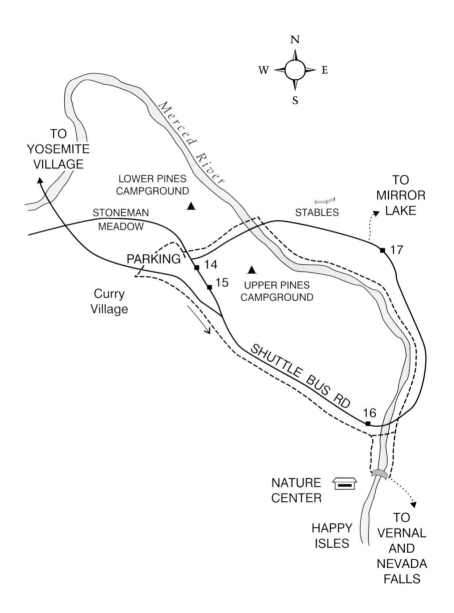

EAST VALLEY LOOP

Hike 5
Lower Yosemite Fall

Hiking distance: 0.5 miles round trip from parking lot
1.5 miles round trip from visitor center
Hiking time: 20 to 45 minutes
Elevation gain: Level
Topo: U.S.G.S. Half Dome and Yosemite Falls

Summary of hike: This short, level trail leads to the base of North America's tallest waterfall. The falls drops 2,425 feet, nearly a half mile, in three tiers from the steep granite cliffs. The trail leads to a bridge crossing Yosemite Creek. Late in the summer, as the amount of water from the falls decreases, the creek bed has a series of small pools and cascades that are popular for soaking and sunbathing (photo on page 27).

Driving directions: Park in the Yosemite Falls parking lot 0.5 miles west of the Yosemite Valley Visitor Center. If the lot is full, park across the road in the Yosemite Lodge parking lot. By shuttle bus, this is Stop No. 7. You may also walk from the Yosemite Valley Visitor Center for an enjoyable 1.5 mile hike.

Hiking directions: From the Yosemite Falls parking lot, walk north on the wide, paved trail. The long, narrow falls is framed by the tall evergreens lining the path. At a quarter mile is a viewing area and bridge that crosses Yosemite Creek. When the spring thaw subsides, visitors scramble up the boulders towards the base of the falls. There are hundreds of pools and gentle cascades among the boulders. To return, retrace your steps. You may also continue past the bridge, staying on the trail which loops back to the parking lot.

If you are starting from the visitor center, take the bike path west to the Yosemite Falls parking lot, and continue north on the paved trail.

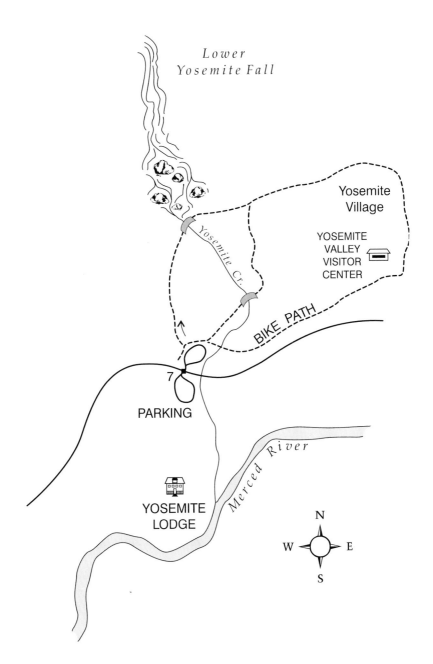

Lower Yosemite Fall

Yosemite Village

YOSEMITE VALLEY VISITOR CENTER

Yosemite Cr.

BIKE PATH

7

PARKING

Merced River

YOSEMITE LODGE

N
W E
S

LOWER YOSEMITE FALL

Hike 6
Bridalveil Fall

Hiking distance: 1.2 miles round trip
Hiking time: 45 minutes
Elevation gain: 100 feet
Topo: U.S.G.S. El Capitan

Summary of hike: Bridalveil Fall is a misty, free-falling waterfall resembling a veil when it is blown by the breezes. Its ribbon of water drops 620 feet off a vertical cliff from the "hanging valley" above to the boulders below. This short, one-mile hike leads to Vista Point, a viewing area with a log bench near the base of Bridalveil Fall. The hike continues across three branches of Bridalveil Creek via stone bridges to a view of the towering El Capitan across the valley floor.

Driving directions: From the west end of Yosemite Valley, the Bridalveil Fall parking lot is located on Highway 41/Wawona Road, 100 feet south of the intersection of Highway 41 and Southside Drive.

Hiking directions: The wide, paved hiking trail begins at the east end of the parking lot. Follow the trail about 200 feet to a junction. Take the trail to the right, leading gently uphill alongside Bridalveil Creek, to Vista Point. A boulder field separates Vista Point from the base of the falls.

When you are finished viewing the falls from Vista Point, head back to the junction. Instead of returning to the parking lot on the left, continue to the right. Cross the three stone bridges over Bridalveil Creek. The trail curves left to a trail junction a short distance before reaching Southside Drive, the valley loop road. From the junction is a picture-perfect view of El Capitan on the north wall of the valley. This is also our turnaround spot. Return along the same path.

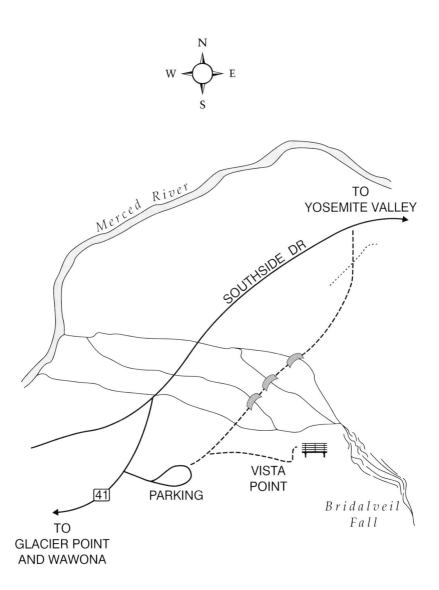

BRIDALVEIL FALL

Hike 7
Bridalveil Creek

Hiking distance: 7 miles round trip
Hiking time: 3 hours
Elevation gain: Near level
Topo: U.S.G.S. Half Dome

Summary of hike: This level trail parallels Bridalveil Creek through the lodgepole pine woods and meadows. It is a quiet, away-from-the-crowds hike. There are an abundance of wildflowers along the meadows and two creek crossings. The trail is also a popular cross-country ski trail during the winter leading to a hut at Ostrander Lake. Two miles downstream from this hike, Bridalveil Creek produces Bridalveil Fall.

Driving directions: From the west end of Yosemite Valley, drive 9 miles south on Highway 41/Wawona Road to Glacier Point Road. Turn left (east) and continue 9.1 miles to the Ostrander Lake Trail parking pullout on the right. The posted pullout is 1.3 miles past the Bridalveil Campground.

Hiking directions: From the Ostrander Lake Trailhead, walk south through the lodgepole pine forest. At 0.2 miles, a wooden footbridge crosses a tributary of Bridalveil Creek. Continue 1.4 miles to a trail junction. Take the right fork leading to the Bridalveil Creek Campground. (The left fork heads to Ostrander Lake.) The trail descends and crosses Bridalveil Creek using boulders as stepping stones. A short distance past the creek is another junction. Again, take the right fork. The trail parallels Bridalveil Creek to the Bridalveil Campground, 1.7 miles from the junction. To return, follow the same trail back. If you prefer a one-way hike, leave a second vehicle at the campground.

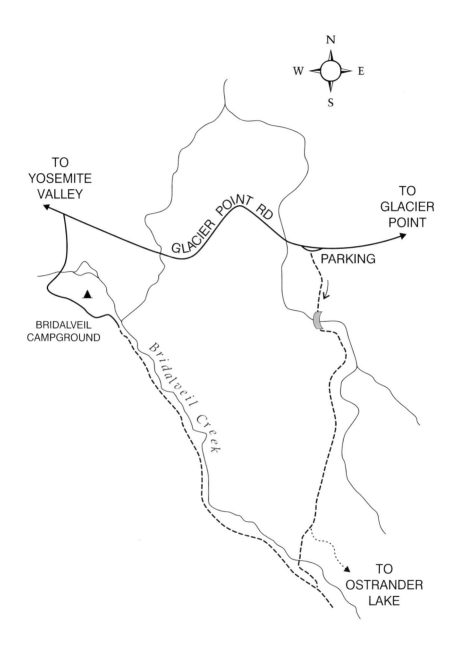

BRIDALVEIL CREEK

Hike 8
Taft Point and The Fissures

Hiking distance: 2.2 miles round trip
Hiking time: 1.5 hours
Elevation gain: 250 feet
Topo: U.S.G.S. Half Dome

Summary of hike: Taft Point is a rocky knoll that overhangs Yosemite Valley from 3,500 feet above (back cover photo). The Fissures on Profile Cliff are fractures in the overhanging cliff, creating crevasses in the rock hundreds of feet deep. These deep and narrow chasms and Taft Point are absolutely stunning. This area has truly spectacular views of Yosemite Valley, including El Capitan, Three Brothers, and Yosemite Falls.

Driving directions: From the west end of Yosemite Valley, drive 9 miles south on Highway 41/Wawona Road to Glacier Point Road. Turn left and continue 13.4 miles to the trailhead parking lot on the left side of the road.

Hiking directions: From the parking lot, the trail heads northwest to a trail junction 150 feet ahead. Take the trail to the left. Taft Point is 1.1 miles ahead. (The trail to the right leads to Sentinel Dome, Hike 9.) A short distance from the junction is a beautiful, white quartz outcropping. The trail descends and crosses Sentinel Creek, the source of Sentinel Fall. Continue through the forest to a junction 0.6 miles from the trailhead. Take the left trail through a shaded grove lush with ferns. (The right fork, the Pohono Trail, leads to Glacier Point.) As you approach The Fissures and Taft Point, the trail heads downhill. You will first approach The Fissures. There are no railings. Falling could be deadly—use caution. To the west is a pipe railing fence at the end of Taft Point. From this open, elevated perch, choose your own route. This is an amazing and unique area to walk around and explore. Return along the same trail.

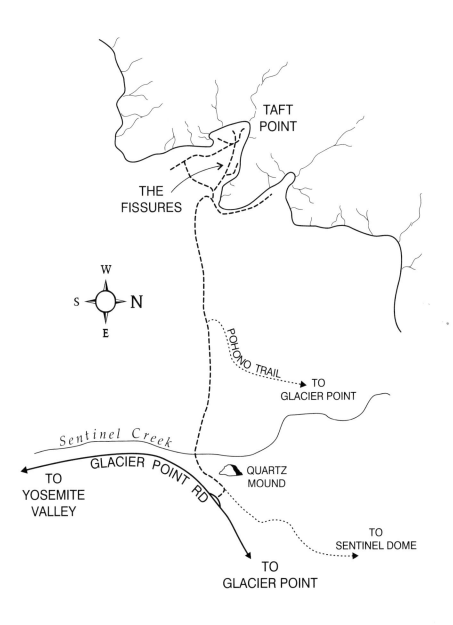

TAFT POINT

THE FISSURES

W N S E

POHONO TRAIL

TO GLACIER POINT

Sentinel Creek

GLACIER POINT RD

TO YOSEMITE VALLEY

QUARTZ MOUND

TO SENTINEL DOME

TO GLACIER POINT

TAFT POINT
AND
THE FISSURES

Vernal Fall - Hike 1

Bridge across Lyell Fork Tuolumne River - Hike 24

Pools at the base of Yosemite Falls – Hike 5

Half Dome – Hike 10

Hike 9
Sentinel Dome

Hiking distance: 2.4 miles round trip
Hiking time: 1.5 hours
Elevation gain: 400 feet
Topo: U.S.G.S. Half Dome

Summary of hike: Sentinel Dome offers one of the highest views of Yosemite Valley, second only to Half Dome. Sitting at 8,122 feet and 4,000 feet above the valley floor, Sentinel Dome has a sweeping 360-degree view of Nevada Fall, Liberty Cap, Half Dome, Clouds Rest, Cathedral Rocks, Yosemite Falls, El Capitan, and the surrounding mountain ranges. The unobstructed views are breathtaking in every direction.

Driving directions: From the west end of Yosemite Valley, drive 9 miles south on Highway 41/Wawona Road, to Glacier Point Road. Turn left and continue 13.4 miles to the trailhead parking lot on the left side of the road.

Hiking directions: From the parking lot, the trail heads northwest to a trail junction 150 feet ahead. Take the trail to the right, towards Sentinel Dome 1.1 miles ahead. (The trail to the left leads to Taft Point, Hike 8.) Sentinel Dome dances in and out of view as the trail leads through open stands of evergreens. As you approach the south base of Sentinel Dome, cairns (man-made rock mounds) keep you on the trail across the open granite. The trail merges with the old, abandoned asphalt road. Follow the road around the east side of the dome to the north face. This side not only overlooks Yosemite Valley, it has the least demanding slope to the dome top. Climb southwest, choosing your own route, up the granite slope to the summit. Explore the perimeter of the dome for the ever-changing views from the peaks to the valleys. Return along the same route.

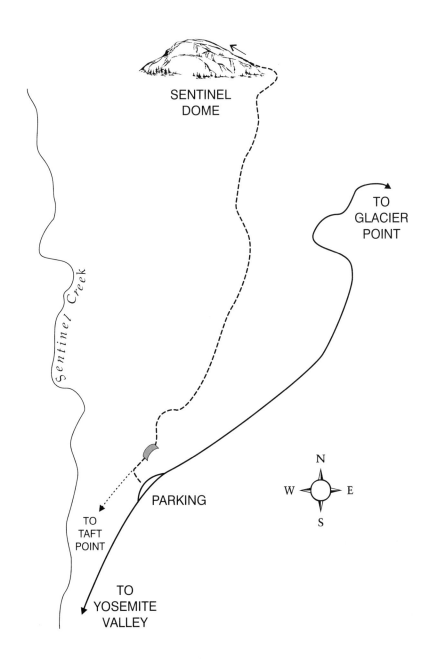

SENTINEL DOME

TO GLACIER POINT

Sentinel Creek

SENTINEL DOME

PARKING

TO TAFT POINT

TO YOSEMITE VALLEY

N
W E
S

SENTINEL DOME

Unicorn Creek enroute to Elizabeth Lake - Hike 21

Giant sequoias in Merced Grove - Hike 12

Gaylor Lakes - Hike 25

Sentinel Rock on the Four-Mile Trail - Hike 10

Hike 10
Four-Mile Trail

Hiking distance: 4.8 miles to valley floor
Hiking time: 2.5 hours
Elevation loss: 3,200 feet
Topo: U.S.G.S. Half Dome

Summary of hike: The Four-Mile Trail is actually 4.8 miles. It begins at Glacier Point overlooking the sculptured landscape of Yosemite Valley. The trail descends 3,200 feet along the south canyon wall via switchbacks to the valley floor. This was the original route to Glacier Point before the road was built. The Four-Mile Trail begins with views up the east side of the valley towards Little Yosemite Valley, Nevada Fall, Vernal Fall, Liberty Cap, Half Dome (photo on page 27), and Tenaya Canyon. Along the trail the views open up to the west, including Sentinel Rock (photo on page 31), Cathedral Rocks, El Capitan, Yosemite Falls, Royal Arches, and the Merced River.

Driving directions: Take the tour bus from Yosemite Lodge (leaving three times daily) one-way to Glacier Point.
　　You may also drive, but a shuttle car is needed. From the west end of Yosemite Valley, drive 9 miles south on Highway 41/Wawona Road to Glacier Point Road. Turn left (east) and continue 16 miles to the Glacier Point parking lot. The shuttle car should be at the trail's end in the valley on Southside Drive at road marker V18, 1.2 miles west of Yosemite Village.

Hiking directions: The trailhead is located at the east end of the parking lot behind the concession building. The trail is well marked and immediately begins its descent through a sugar pine and white fir forest. There are no trail junctions. Once you begin the descent along the cliff, angling down into the valley, it is a nonstop visual treat. Use Sentinel Rock, which is frequently in view, as a gauge to measure your descent.

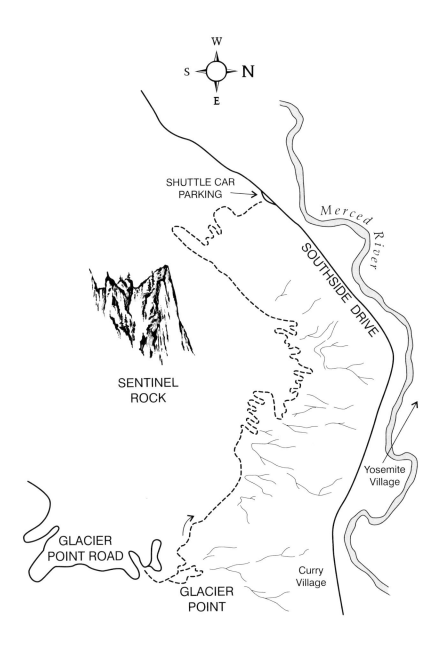

W
S — N
E

SHUTTLE CAR
PARKING

Merced River

SOUTHSIDE DRIVE

SENTINEL
ROCK

Yosemite
Village

GLACIER
POINT ROAD

Curry
Village

GLACIER
POINT

FOUR-MILE TRAIL

Hike 11
Mariposa Grove of Giant Sequoias

Summary of hike: Yosemite National Park has three giant sequoia groves. Of these three, the Mariposa Grove of Giant Sequoias is the largest and most visited. It is divided into two groves—Upper Grove and Lower Grove. Some of these giant sequoias are believed to be nearly 3,000 years old. Their average height is 250 feet, with a base diameter of 15 to 20 feet and bark two feet thick. Their shallow roots are only 3 to 6 feet deep but extend outwards up to 150 feet to support the massive tree. They are among the oldest and largest living things on earth and are resistant to disease, insects, and fire. Mariposa Grove has an impressive display of more than 500 mature giant sequoias within its 250-acre area. One of the largest and oldest trees in this grove is the Grizzly Giant, estimated to be 2,700 years old with a height of 200 feet and a 30-foot diameter.

The area has a network of trails with posted junctions that allow a variety of routes. I have chosen two different hikes. The first is through the Lower Grove only. It is 2.2 miles round trip with a 400-foot elevation gain. Information plaques are placed along the trail. The trail visits the Grizzly Giant, California Tunnel Tree, Bachelor and Three Graces, and Fallen Monarch.

The second hike takes the tram up to the Mariposa Grove Museum in the Upper Grove. It is a one-way, 2.5-mile trip that descends through both groves back to the parking lot. This trail enables you to see all of the trees in the first hike, plus the Fallen Wawona Tree, Telescope Tree, Columbia Tree, Clothespin Tree, and Faithful Couple. The hike also allows a visit to the museum and a quiet walk through the forest. Whichever hike or side trails you choose, the area is beautiful and rewarding.

Driving and hiking directions for the Mariposa Grove trails are found on pages 36—37.

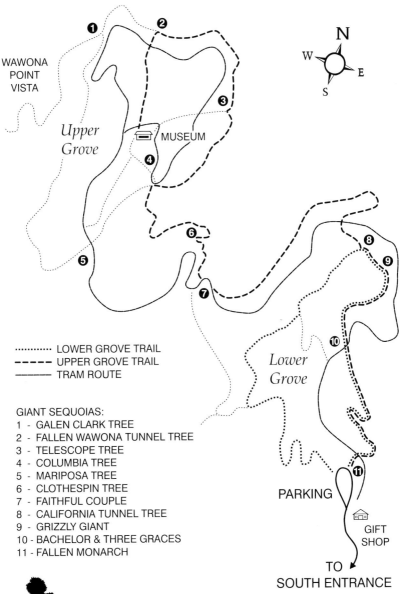

WAWONA
POINT
VISTA

Upper Grove

MUSEUM

N
W   E
S

Lower Grove

············ LOWER GROVE TRAIL
------- UPPER GROVE TRAIL
——— TRAM ROUTE

GIANT SEQUOIAS:
1 - GALEN CLARK TREE
2 - FALLEN WAWONA TUNNEL TREE
3 - TELESCOPE TREE
4 - COLUMBIA TREE
5 - MARIPOSA TREE
6 - CLOTHESPIN TREE
7 - FAITHFUL COUPLE
8 - CALIFORNIA TUNNEL TREE
9 - GRIZZLY GIANT
10 - BACHELOR & THREE GRACES
11 - FALLEN MONARCH

PARKING

GIFT
SHOP

TO
SOUTH ENTRANCE

MARIPOSA GROVE
OF
GIANT SEQUOIAS

Lower Mariposa Grove

Hiking distance: 2.2 mile loop
Hiking time: 1 hour
Elevation gain: 400 feet
Topo: U.S.G.S. Mariposa Grove

Driving directions: From the west end of Yosemite Valley, drive 28.5 miles south on Highway 41/Wawona Road to the Mariposa Grove parking lot located at the end of the road. It is 6.8 miles past Wawona and two miles east of the south entrance turnoff. A free shuttle to the Mariposa Grove is available from Wawona.

Hiking directions: A map of this hike is found on page 35. The trailhead is at the end of the parking lot next to the sign and map dispenser. Take the trail a short distance to the Fallen Monarch tree. After the Fallen Monarch is a footbridge and the tram road. Cross the road and continue gently uphill on the rock steps to Bachelor and Three Graces. The Three Graces are grouped together while the Bachelor is off on his own. Again cross the tram road to the trail alongside a stream, and continue to the Grizzly Giant. The trail circles the Grizzly Giant and heads west about 50 yards to the California Tunnel Tree. A tunnel was cut through the tree in 1895 to accommodate the growing tourist industry. Take the southwest trail that leads to Wawona. At the second junction on the left, head back to the parking lot, completing the loop. (The first junction leads back to Bachelor and Three Graces.)

Upper and Lower Mariposa Grove
via tram ride to
Mariposa Grove Museum

Hiking distance: 2.5 miles one-way return
Hiking time: 1.5 hours
Elevation loss: 1,000 feet
Topo: U.S.G.S. Mariposa Grove

Driving directions: Follow the same driving directions for Lower Mariposa Grove on the previous page.

Hiking directions: A map of this hike is found on page 35. The open-air tram departs from the gift shop near the parking lot every 20 minutes. It winds 2.5 miles through the Lower Grove to the Upper Grove. The drivers stop along the way and share information about the trees and history of the area.

Depart the tram at the Mariposa Grove Museum. After visiting the museum, head north 0.3 miles to the Fallen Wawona Tunnel Tree. This tree was tunneled out in 1881 and fell in 1969. Head east along the Outer Loop Trail down to Telescope Tree, hollowed by fire, yet still alive. Continue downhill to Columbia Tree near a four-way junction. Take the south trail downhill past Clothespin Tree to the tram road. The road is adjacent to Faithful Couple, two separate trees fused together at their bases. From here, go left along the tram road a short distance, and pick up the trail going to the north, which intersects with the Lower Grove Trail at Grizzly Giant and California Tunnel Tree. Continue south, passing Bachelor and Three Graces and Fallen Monarch back to the parking lot.

Hike 12
Merced Grove of Giant Sequoias

Hiking distance: 4 miles round trip
Hiking time: 2 hours
Elevation gain: 400 feet
Topo: U.S.G.S. El Portal

Summary of hike: Yosemite has three giant sequoia groves. Merced Grove is the smallest and least visited. It is a dense, natural forest uninterrupted by development. About twenty giant sequoias are scattered through this area (photo on page 30). This is not a populated trail, so you will have an opportunity to enjoy a quiet and secluded tour of these magnificent trees. A stream runs through the forest in the canyon.

Driving directions: From the west end of Yosemite Valley, drive west towards Highway 120. From the Highway 120/140 junction, take Highway 120 for 13.3 miles to the Merced Grove parking lot on the left. It is located 3.5 miles past the Crane Flat Campground. A trailhead sign is posted.

From Tuolumne Meadows, drive southwest to the end of Tioga Road. Turn right on Highway 120. Continue 3.7 miles to the Merced Grove parking lot on the left.

Hiking directions: From the parking lot, head south through a beautifully forested area along an old gravel fire road. At 0.75 miles is a trail fork. Take the left fork and pass the gate. For the next mile the trail descends along the curving road to the canyon floor. At the bottom of the hill, the trail curves to the left. At this curve are six giant sequoias. From here, sequoias are sprinkled throughout the forest. The Russell Cabin or Merced Grove Cabin sits in the grove to the right. Several side trails lead down to the stream and past more giant sequoias. Although the trail continues down canyon, this is our turn-around spot. Return along the same route.

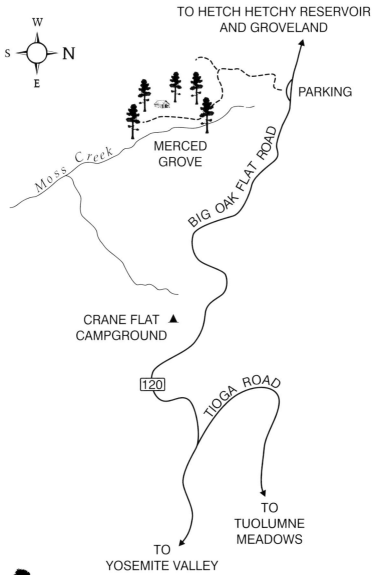

TO HETCHY HETCHY RESERVOIR
AND GROVELAND

PARKING

MERCED
GROVE

Moss Creek

BIG OAK FLAT ROAD

CRANE FLAT ▲
CAMPGROUND

120

TIOGA ROAD

TO
TUOLUMNE
MEADOWS

TO
YOSEMITE VALLEY

MERCED GROVE
OF
GIANT SEQUOIAS

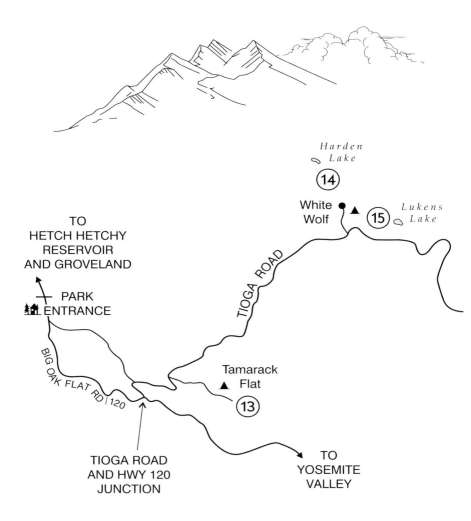

Harden Lake

(14)

White Wolf ● ▲ (15) *Lukens Lake*

TO
HETCH HETCHY
RESERVOIR
AND GROVELAND

TIOGA ROAD

PARK
ENTRANCE

BIG OAK FLAT RD | 120

Tamarack
▲ Flat
(13)

TIOGA ROAD
AND HWY 120
JUNCTION

TO
YOSEMITE
VALLEY

N
W · E
S

TO
LEE VINING

Dog Lake

25

Gaylor Lakes

TUOLUMNE MEADOWS

22

23

20

May Lake

16

TUOLUMNE LODGE

24

TUOLUMNE VISITOR CENTER

17

Tenaya Lake

19

Cathedral Lake

21

Elizabeth Lake

18

Sunrise Lakes

TIOGA ROAD
HIKES 13 – 25

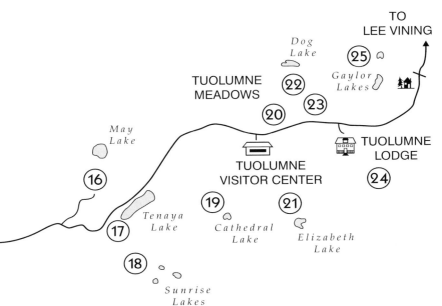

Hike 13
Cascade Creek

Hiking distance: 5 miles round trip
Hiking time: 2.5 hours
Elevation gain: 350 feet
Topo: U.S.G.S. Tamarack Flat and El Capitan

Summary of hike: The trail to Cascade Creek is a quiet, secluded hike along the original Big Oak Flat Road that led to Yosemite Valley back in 1874. The abandoned road has been closed to vehicles since landslides blocked its path in 1945. The trail passes through a cedar, fir, and pine forest, paralleling a tributary of Cascade Creek to a bridge crossing Cascade Creek. The creek has pools for swimming near the bridge.

Driving directions: From the Tioga Road and Highway 120 junction, take the Tioga Road 3.7 miles east to the Tamarack Campground turnoff on the right. Turn right and drive 3 miles to the end of the poorly maintained road. Park where available.

From the Tuolumne Visitor Center, drive 34.8 miles west to the Tamarack Campground turnoff on the left. Turn left and follow the directions above.

Hiking directions: The trailhead is at the south end of the campground. Walk past the gate to an old asphalt road that leads through the forest. At 0.5 miles, the trail crosses Tamarack Creek. At one mile the trail begins its descent. The display of boulders in this area is magnificent. The trail crosses a tributary of Cascade Creek, then follows the creek downstream to the bridge crossing Cascade Creek. The creek has various cascades and swimming holes the last quarter mile before reaching the bridge. Although the trail continues beyond the bridge, this is our turnaround spot. Return along the same trail.

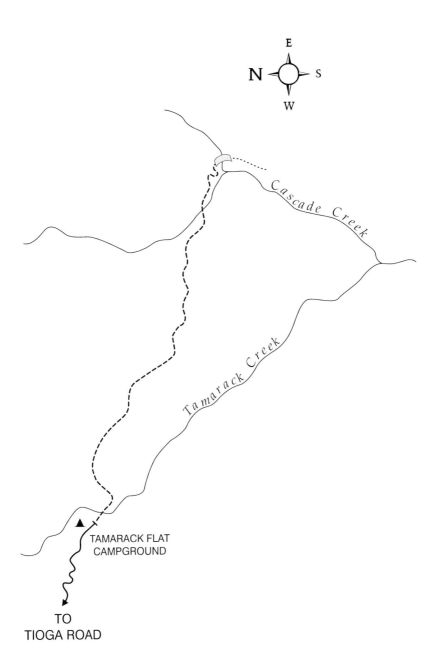

N E S W

Cascade Creek

Tamarack Creek

TAMARACK FLAT
CAMPGROUND

TO
TIOGA ROAD

CASCADE CREEK

Hike 14
Harden Lake

Hiking distance: 6 miles round trip
Hiking time: 3 hours
Elevation gain: 450 feet
Topo: U.S.G.S. Tamarack Flat and Hetch Hetchy Reservoir

Summary of hike: The trail to Harden Lake follows the original Tioga Road built in 1883. It was closed to vehicles in 1961 when the current Tioga Road was completed. The hike parallels the Middle Fork of the Tuolumne River downstream through a beautiful pine forest. The river contains small cascades and a variety of swimming holes. Harden Lake, at an elevation of 7,600 feet, is a popular, yet not crowded, fishing and picnicking spot.

Driving directions: From the Tioga Road and Highway 120 junction, take the Tioga Road 14.5 miles east to the White Wolf Campground turnoff on the left. Turn left and drive one mile to the White Wolf Lodge. Park near the lodge.

From the Tuolumne Visitor Center, drive 24 miles west to the White Wolf Campground turnoff on the right. Turn right and follow the directions above.

Hiking directions: From White Wolf Lodge, walk down the road to the north, passing the campground. The road (no longer accessible to vehicles) crosses a bridge over the Middle Fork of the Tuolumne River. For the next mile the trail parallels the east bank of the river. At 1.6 miles a posted footpath to Harden Lake branches off to the right. You may stay on the road or take the footpath. They connect again 0.3 miles before reaching Harden Lake. If you choose the road, there is another fork in the road 0.3 miles past the footpath junction. Take the trail to the right. A "Harden Lake" sign is posted. (The left trail continues along the original Tioga Road to the park boundary near the Big Oak Flat entrance.) As you approach the south end of Harden Lake, there is a trail junction. Take the right fork descending to the lake. From here, you can explore the perimeter of the lake. Return along the same trail.

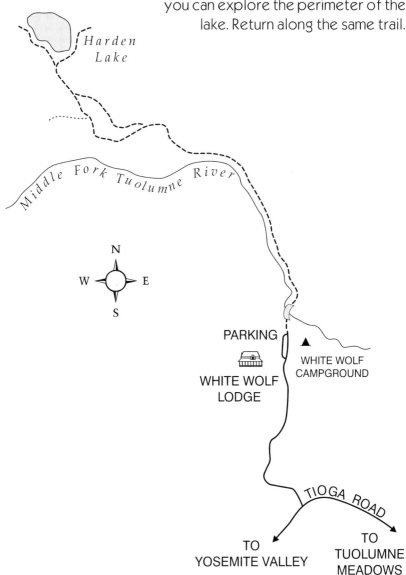

HARDEN LAKE

Hike 15
Lukens Lake - two routes

Hiking distance: 4.6 miles round trip and 1.6 miles round trip
Hiking time: 2.5 hours and 1 hour
Elevation gain: 250 feet and 150 feet
Topo: U.S.G.S. Tamarack Flat and Yosemite Falls

Summary of hike: Lukens Lake is a scenic mountain lake forested along the north and west sides. To the south and east of the lake are beautiful meadows covered in wildflowers. There are two trails leading to the lake. Both trails are easy hikes and lead through lush forests. The map includes the trails from both directions. The longer route begins at White Wolf Lodge. The shorter route begins along the Tioga Road.

Driving directions: To start from White Wolf Lodge, follow the same driving directions as Hike 14, parking near the lodge.
     The trailhead for the shorter hike is located on Tioga Road 1.8 miles east of the White Wolf turnoff. Park on the south side of the road. From the Tuolumne Visitor Center, the trailhead is located 22 miles west on Tioga Road.

Hiking directions: The posted trailhead at White Wolf is directly across the road from the lodge. The trail heads east through a lodgepole pine forest along the south edge of the campground. At 0.7 miles is a log crossing over the Middle Fork of the Tuolumne River. At 0.9 miles is a posted trail junction. Take the right fork, which parallels the river for the next mile to another junction. Again take the right fork and cross the river. Continue uphill to the north shore of Lukens Lake. The trail parallels the lake along the east shore and joins the shorter Lukens Lake trail from Tioga Road. To return, retrace your steps.
     From the pullout on Tioga Road, the trail heads across the highway to a forested ridge. It then descends to a meadow at the south end of Lukens Lake, joining the longer trail from the north.

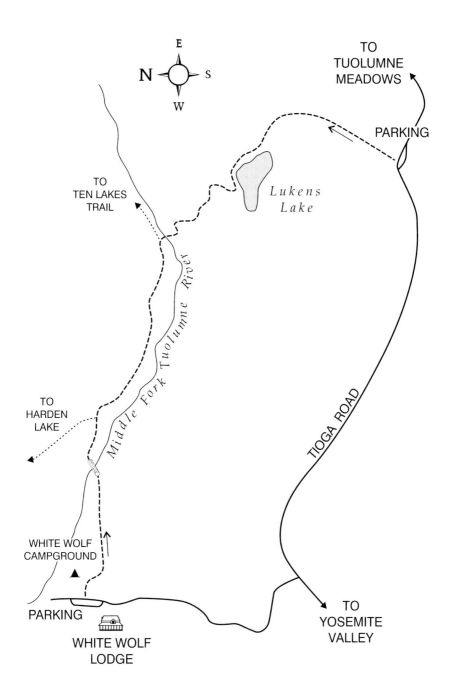

N E S W

TO
TUOLUMNE
MEADOWS

PARKING

TO
TEN LAKES
TRAIL

Lukens Lake

Middle Fork Tuolumne River

TO
HARDEN
LAKE

TIOGA ROAD

WHITE WOLF
CAMPGROUND

TO
YOSEMITE
VALLEY

PARKING

WHITE WOLF
LODGE

LUKENS LAKE

Hike 16
May Lake

Hiking distance: 2.4 miles round trip
Hiking time: 1.5 hours
Elevation gain: 400 feet
Topo: U.S.G.S. Tenaya Lake

Summary of hike: May Lake is nestled beneath the towering eastern wall of Mount Hoffman. Located in the center of Yosemite, Mount Hoffman rises more than 1,500 feet out of May Lake to a height of 10,850 feet. The forested lake is home to the May Lake High Sierra Camp. The trail offers views across Tenaya Canyon and Cathedral Peak to the east and to Half Dome and Clouds Rest to the south. May Lake is a popular trout fishing lake.

Driving directions: From the Tioga Road and Highway 120 junction, take Tioga Road 27 miles east to the May Lake turnoff on the left. Turn left and drive 1.8 miles to the trailhead parking lot at the end of the road.

From the Tuolumne Visitor Center, drive 11.4 miles west to the May Lake turnoff on the right. Turn right and follow the directions above.

Hiking directions: The trailhead is to the southwest (left) of Snow Pond. Cross the bridge and begin hiking north. The trail steadily gains elevation, but is not steep. The trail passes through an open forest dominated by pine and fir, allowing plenty of sunlight to filter in through the trees. Portions of the trail cross large slabs of granite dotted with lodgepole pines. Just before reaching May Lake is a trail fork. The left fork leads to the south end of the lake by the backpackers' camping area. The right fork follows the east side of the lake, passing the tent cabins of the May Lake High Sierra Camp. Although the trail continues into the backcountry to Ten Lakes and Glen Aulin, May Lake is our turnaround spot. Return along the same trail.

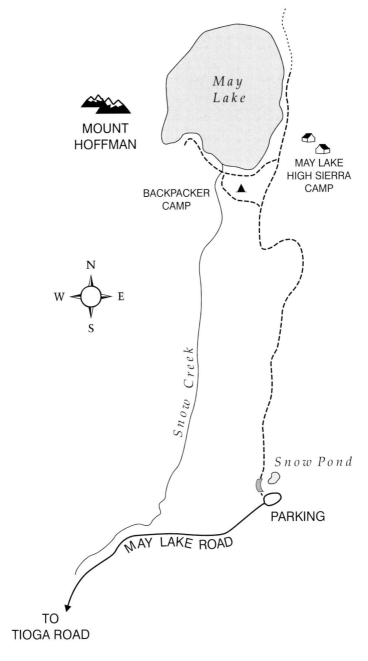

MOUNT HOFFMAN

May Lake

MAY LAKE HIGH SIERRA CAMP

BACKPACKER CAMP

N
W E
S

Snow Creek

Snow Pond

PARKING

MAY LAKE ROAD

TO
TIOGA ROAD

MAY LAKE

Hike 17
Tenaya Lake

Hiking distance: 2.6 miles round trip
Hiking time: 1.5 hours
Elevation gain: Level
Topo: U.S.G.S. Tenaya Lake

Summary of hike: This hike begins at the mile-long Tenaya Lake and follows the southeast shore. Along the north shore, Polly Dome, the steep-sloped granite rock, rises 1,600 feet above the lake. To the east, Tenaya Peak towers above. The lake has several sandy beaches, including a quarter-mile beach and picnic area along the northeast shore.

Driving directions: From the Tioga Road and Highway 120 junction, take Tioga Road 31 miles east to the parking lot on the right at the southwest end of Tenaya Lake. This is the site of the now-closed Tenaya Lake Campground.

From the Tuolumne Visitor Center the parking lot is 7.7 miles west on the left.

Hiking directions: The trail begins at the southwest end of Tenaya Lake. Head east along the road towards Tenaya Creek, the Tenaya Lake outlet. After crossing, take the trail to the left, staying close to the south shore of Tenaya Lake. (The trail to the right heads to the Sunrise Lakes, Hike 18.) The trail follows closely to the perimeter of the lake through a forest. At the north end of the lake is Tenaya Creek again, the lake's inlet. Cross the creek to the sandy beach along the northeast side of the lake. From the beach, return by taking the same trail back. The views of the surrounding mountains are equally rewarding on the return trip.

You may also complete the loop around the lake instead of backtracking. A portion of the trail is on Tioga Road, which makes the loop less appealing.

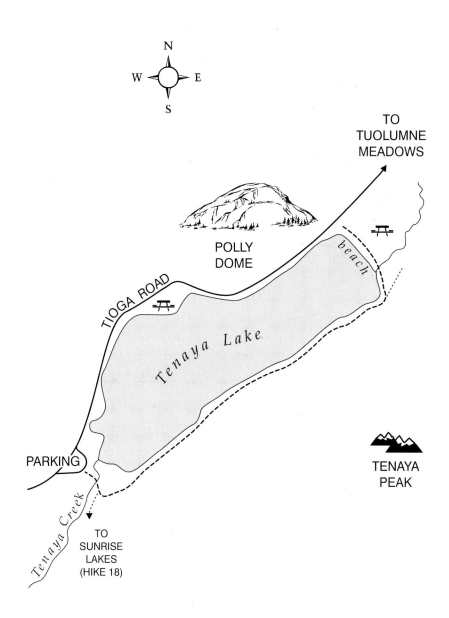

N
W E
S

TO
TUOLUMNE
MEADOWS

POLLY
DOME

beach

TIOGA ROAD

Tenaya Lake

TENAYA
PEAK

PARKING

Tenaya Creek

TO
SUNRISE
LAKES
(HIKE 18)

TENAYA LAKE

Hike 18
Sunrise Lakes

Hiking distance: 8 miles round trip
Hiking time: 4—5 hours
Elevation gain: 1,000 feet
Topo: U.S.G.S. Tenaya Lake

Summary of hike: The Sunrise Lakes are a series of three, beautiful mountain lakes. The trail has a steep, one-mile ascent in which most of the elevation gain is achieved. There are dramatic panoramic views along the way. From the top is a unique view of Half Dome and Yosemite Valley.

Driving directions: Same as Tenaya Lake, Hike 17.

Hiking directions: The trail begins at the southwest end of Tenaya Lake. Head east along the road towards Tenaya Creek. After crossing, take the trail to the right, descending into Tenaya Canyon through a forest parallel to Tenaya Creek. At all the posted trail junctions, head towards "Sunrise H.S.C.," the High Sierra Camp located beyond the lakes. At 1.5 miles the trail begins a steep climb out of the canyon, gaining more than 800 feet in one mile via a series of switchbacks. At the top, the trail to the left leads to the Sunrise Lakes. First, take a short detour to the right along an unmarked trail. About 300 yards ahead is a commanding view of Yosemite Valley and Half Dome.

Back at the junction, it is an easy half mile to the first of the lakes. The trail winds along the west shore of Lower Sunrise Lake, crossing the lake's outlet stream. In the next mile, the trail continues gently uphill to the middle and upper lakes. The middle lake is off to the left—a short spur trail will lead you there. The main trail skirts along the southwest shore of Upper Sunrise Lake. Although the trail continues to the Sunrise High Sierra Camp 1.5 miles further, the third Sunrise Lake is our turnaround area. To return, retrace your steps.

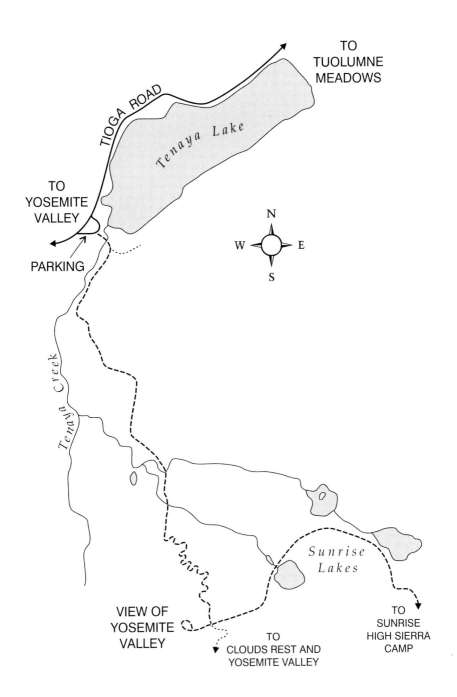

TO
TUOLUMNE
MEADOWS

TIOGA ROAD

Tenaya Lake

TO
YOSEMITE
VALLEY

PARKING

N

W E

S

Tenaya Creek

Sunrise Lakes

VIEW OF
YOSEMITE
VALLEY

TO
CLOUDS REST AND
YOSEMITE VALLEY

TO
SUNRISE
HIGH SIERRA
CAMP

SUNRISE LAKES

Hike 19
Lower Cathedral Lake

Hiking distance: 7 miles round trip
Hiking time: 4 hours
Elevation gain: 1,000 feet
Topo: U.S.G.S. Tenaya Lake

Summary of hike: Lower Cathedral Lake sits at 9,250 feet in a bowl beneath the shadow of Cathedral Peak. Glaciated mountains curve around the southwest side of the lake, while bedrock surrounds the lake's perimeter. This subalpine trail up to the lake has views of the Tenaya Lake basin and the smooth, bare Fairview Dome. This trail is part of the John Muir Trail.

Driving directions: From the Tuolumne Visitor Center, drive 0.5 miles west on Tioga Road to the trailhead parking lot on the left (south) side of the road.

Hiking directions: From the parking lot, the trail heads southwest to a junction at 0.1 mile. Continue along the same trail straight ahead. The trail climbs 550 feet through the forest in 0.7 miles, then levels off for a half mile. At this point, the trail skirts the base of Cathedral Peak's northern granite slope. At 1.4 miles the trail crosses Cathedral Creek. After crossing the creek, the trail begins its second ascent, gaining 450 feet in a half mile. As the trail levels, the route passes through an open, sandy forest, while the spires of Cathedral Peak come into full view. At three miles is a fork. Take the right branch to Lower Cathedral Lake, 0.5 miles ahead. (The left fork continues along the John Muir Trail to Yosemite Valley, passing Upper Cathedral Lake.) The trail zigzags down the rocky slope, crossing a stream three times to a meadow. Several trails cross the meadow to the east shore of the lake. Choose your own path as you explore. On the west side are views down the valley to Tenaya Lake and Polly Dome. Return along the same trail.

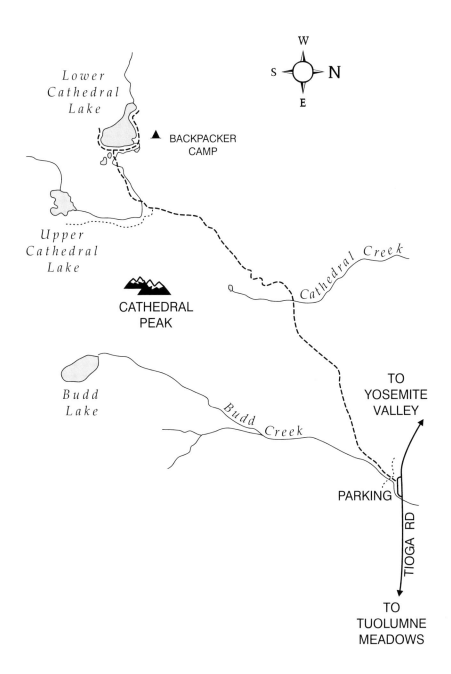

Lower
Cathedral
Lake

▲ BACKPACKER
CAMP

Upper
Cathedral
Lake

CATHEDRAL
PEAK

Cathedral Creek

Budd
Lake

Budd Creek

TO
YOSEMITE
VALLEY

PARKING

TIOGA RD

TO
TUOLUMNE
MEADOWS

W
N
S
E

CATHEDRAL LAKES

Hike 20
Tuolumne Meadows and Soda Springs

Hiking distance: 1.5 miles round trip
Hiking time: 1 hour
Elevation gain: Level
Topo: U.S.G.S. Vogelsang Peak and Tioga Pass

Summary of hike: Tuolumne Meadows, 2.5 miles long, is the largest subalpine meadow in the Sierra Nevada. The meadow was formed by a glacier more than 2,000 feet thick. The Tuolumne River winds through the meadow surrounded by peaks and domes. Soda Springs, located on the north side of the meadow, is a naturally carbonated mineral spring. Pools of mineral water bubble up from beneath the ground. Northwest of Soda Springs is the historic Parsons Memorial Lodge, built entirely from native rock and log in 1915 by the Sierra Club. This hike visits all of these areas, plus crossing a bridge over the Tuolumne River. This lush meadow is a popular area for swimming and picnicking. You can easily spend the whole day exploring and daydreaming in the meadow.

Driving directions: The trailhead is located 0.1 mile east of the Tuolumne Meadows Visitor Center along the north side of Tioga Road. Parking spaces are available alongside the road.

Hiking directions: From the parking area, the wide trail heads north, directly into the meadow. Continue 0.5 miles to a wooden bridge crossing the Tuolumne River—cross the bridge. A trail leads to the left along the river. A short distance ahead is a junction. Take the trail to the right leading up to Parsons Memorial Lodge. From the lodge, a trail leads east to Soda Springs and a wooden structure on a grassy knoll. From the springs the trail heads back down to the Tuolumne River and the bridge. Additional trails meander along the river and through the meadow.

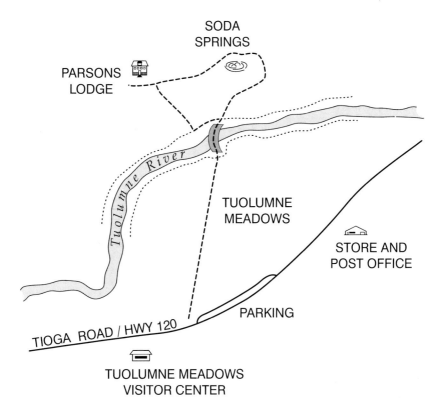

TUOLUMNE MEADOWS
AND
SODA SPRINGS

Hike 21
Elizabeth Lake

Hiking distance: 4.6 miles round trip
Hiking time: 3 hours
Elevation gain: 800 feet
Topo: U.S.G.S. Vogelsang Peak

Summary of hike: The hike to Elizabeth Lake is a steady climb for the first half of the hike. The trail then parallels Unicorn Creek through a beautiful valley (photo on page 30). A lush meadow marbled with streams surrounds the lake. The glacially carved granite cliffs of the Cathedral Range form a cirque around the south end of Elizabeth Lake, while the spire of Unicorn Peak towers above to the west. This is a great place to admire the scenery, picnic, and explore the delicate shoreline.

Driving directions: The trailhead is located inside the Tuolumne Meadows Campground on Tioga Road, one mile east of the Tuolumne Visitor Center. At the campground entrance booth, request a free day-parking permit and campground/trailhead map. The trailhead is located by Campsite B-49.

There is also a trail leading to the trailhead from the Tuolumne Visitor Center. This route would add a mile to your hike in each direction.

Hiking directions: At the trailhead, head south to a junction with the John Muir Trail, 300 feet ahead. Continue south on the main trail. There is a small stream crossing at 0.5 miles and another crossing at one mile. Just past the second stream, the trail levels off. At 1.2 miles the route meets, then parallels, the cascading waters of Unicorn Creek. The trail divides as you approach the lake. The right fork leads through a meadow to the northern portion of Elizabeth Lake. The left fork leads to the southern part of the lake. Footpaths lead in both directions along the shore. To return, follow the same path back.

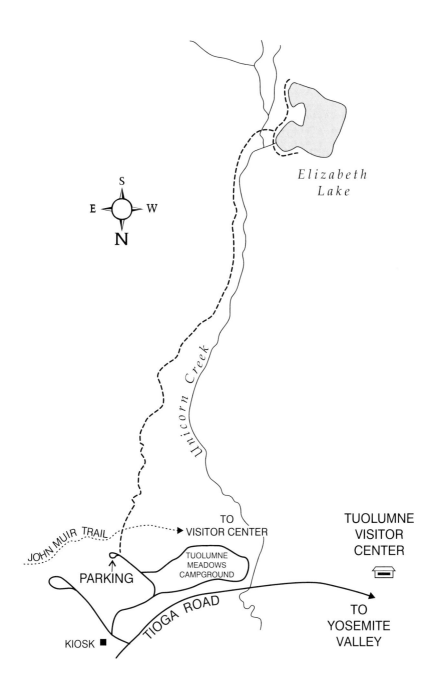

Elizabeth Lake

Unicorn Creek

S
E — W
N

JOHN MUIR TRAIL

TO
VISITOR CENTER

TUOLUMNE
VISITOR
CENTER

TUOLUMNE
MEADOWS
CAMPGROUND

PARKING

TIOGA ROAD

TO
YOSEMITE
VALLEY

KIOSK ■

ELIZABETH LAKE

Hike 22
Dog Lake

Hiking distance: 2.4 miles round trip
Hiking time: 1.5 hours
Elevation gain: 600 feet
Topo: U.S.G.S. Tioga Pass

Summary of hike: Dog Lake, at 9,240 feet, is a beautiful half-mile-long lake surrounded by grassy meadows and stands of lodgepole pines. A smooth, level path circles the lake, while mountain peaks rise up in the distance. The grassy terrain and pretty surroundings make this a great place for a picnic. The trail to Dog Lake leads through a lodgepole pine forest. Although short, the trail is steep at times.

Driving directions: From the Tuolumne Visitor Center, drive 1.2 miles east on Tioga Road to the well-marked trailhead parking lot on the left (north) side of the road.

Hiking directions: From the parking lot, the trail leads north past the restrooms to a trail junction. The Dog Lake Trail goes to the left. (The right trail leads to Lembert Dome, Hike 23.) The trail leads through a small meadow and into the lodgepole forest. From here, the climb begins, gaining 450 feet in the next half mile. As it levels off, there is a stream crossing to another junction—stay left. (The right trail leads to the north side of Lembert Dome.) Continue gently uphill to another junction one mile from the trailhead. Bear to the right. (The left leads to the Young Lakes, 4.9 miles beyond.) From this junction it is 0.2 miles to the west end of Dog Lake. The designated trail leads along the southern shore, although trails lead around the lake in both directions. Return along the same trail.

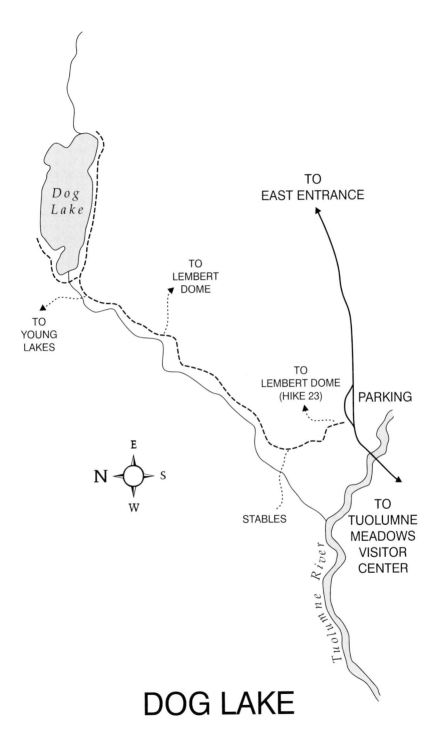

TO
EAST ENTRANCE

Dog Lake

TO
LEMBERT
DOME

TO
YOUNG
LAKES

TO
LEMBERT DOME
(HIKE 23)

PARKING

E

N ⊕ S

W

STABLES

TO
TUOLUMNE
MEADOWS
VISITOR
CENTER

Tuolumne River

DOG LAKE

Hike 23
Lembert Dome

Hiking distance: 2.8 miles round trip
Hiking time: 2 hours
Elevation gain: 850 feet
Topo: U.S.G.S. Tioga Pass

Summary of hike: Lembert Dome is an impressive, polished granite dome sculpted by glacial ice. From its 9,450-foot elevation, it offers the premiere view of Tuolumne Meadows and the canyon below. From the exposed dome summit, there is a sweeping 360-degree view of mountain peaks in every direction. The trail up to the north side of the dome is short but steep. Careful footing, especially on the way down, is essential.

Note: Most of the Yosemite trail maps, including the U.S.G.S. and Trails Illustrated maps, do not show this trail. It is shown on the Tuolumne Meadows and Campground map available at the visitor center and the campground.

Driving directions: From the Tuolumne Visitor Center, drive 1.2 miles east on Tioga Road to the well-marked trailhead parking lot on the left (north) side of the road.

Hiking directions: From the parking lot, the trail leads north past the restrooms. At 0.1 mile is a posted trail junction. Take the right fork to Lembert Dome. (The left fork leads to Dog Lake, Hike 22.) The trail immediately begins its steep ascent through the lodgepole pine forest around the west flank of Lembert Dome. From the saddle along the north side, the ascent up the bald back of the dome itself becomes easier. The dome is not as steep a climb as it appears from below. Choose your own route as you climb south along the dome's bare surface. There are a variety of levels to hike to. From the first hill you are rewarded with spectacular views down canyon. Choose a path to suit your own comfort level. Return along the same trail.

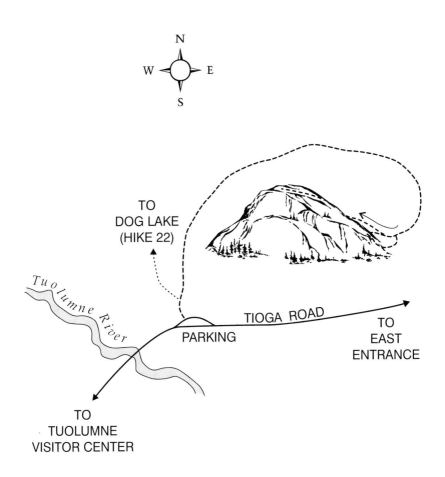

N
W · E
S

TO
DOG LAKE
(HIKE 22)

Tuolumne River

TIOGA ROAD

PARKING

TO
EAST
ENTRANCE

TO
TUOLUMNE
VISITOR CENTER

LEMBERT DOME

Hike 24
Lyell Canyon

Hiking distance: 2.2 miles round trip up to 15 miles
Hiking time: 1 hour or more
Elevation gain: Near level
Topo: U.S.G.S. Vogelsang Peak and Tioga Pass

Summary of hike: Lyell Canyon offers a scenic, pastoral hike along a level portion of the John Muir Trail. The trail passes through beautiful subalpine meadows along the banks of the Lyell Fork of the Tuolumne River. The trail crosses the Dana Fork of the Tuolumne River and a double bridge built into smooth granite slabs over the Lyell Fork (photo on page 26). There are pools and cascades at the double bridge.

Driving directions: The trailhead is by the Tuolumne Meadows Lodge parking lot. Drive 1.6 miles east of the Tuolumne Visitor Center on Tioga Road to the lodge turnoff on the right—turn right. Continue 0.4 miles to the first parking lot on the left.

If you are camping at Tuolumne Meadows Campground, you may begin the hike at the south end of the A-Campsites. The trail parallels the Lyell Fork for one mile to a junction where the two trails meet near the double bridge over the Lyell Fork.

Hiking directions: From the lodge parking lot, cross the road to the trailhead. Walk east, parallel to the Dana Fork, and cross the bridge. Follow the forested trail 0.5 miles to the double bridge crossing. Just beyond the bridge is a trail junction with the John Muir Trail. Take the trail to the left, following the Lyell Fork up Lyell Canyon. (The trail to the right leads back one mile to the Tuolumne Meadows Campground.) A half mile up canyon from the junction is a footbridge that crosses Rafferty Creek. This is the turnaround spot for a 2.2 mile hike.

If you wish to hike further, you can turn around at any point along the canyon.

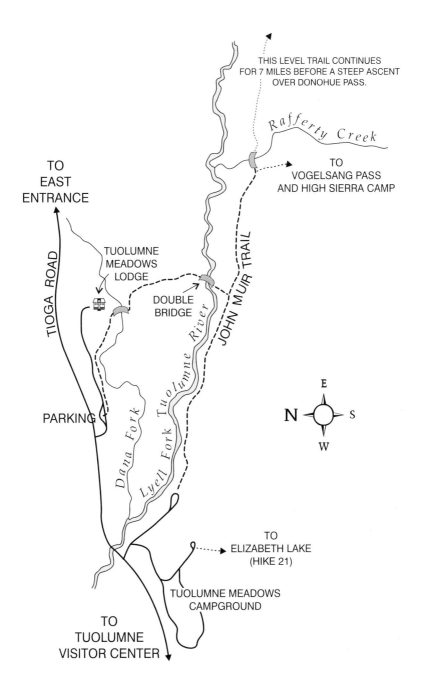

THIS LEVEL TRAIL CONTINUES
FOR 7 MILES BEFORE A STEEP ASCENT
OVER DONOHUE PASS.

Rafferty Creek

TO
EAST
ENTRANCE

TO
VOGELSANG PASS
AND HIGH SIERRA CAMP

TIOGA ROAD

TUOLUMNE
MEADOWS
LODGE

DOUBLE
BRIDGE

Tuolumne River

JOHN MUIR TRAIL

Dana Fork

Lyell Fork

PARKING

E

N — S

W

TO
ELIZABETH LAKE
(HIKE 21)

TUOLUMNE MEADOWS
CAMPGROUND

TO
TUOLUMNE
VISITOR CENTER

LYELL CANYON

Hike 25
Gaylor Lakes

Hiking distance: 4 miles round trip
Hiking time: 3 hours
Elevation gain: 800 feet
Topo: U.S.G.S. Tioga Pass

Summary of hike: The hike to the Gaylor Lakes leads to a high altitude "top of the world" alpine plateau. The lakes sit above 10,000 feet in a treeless meadow teaming with wildflowers, babbling creeks, and an endless panorama of mountain peaks in every direction. The hike includes a visit to a stone cabin, built from native rock without mortar, and the remains of the Great Sierra Mine, built in the late 1870s. From the mine is a magnificent view south of the two lakes and surrounding peaks (photo on page 31).

Driving directions: From the Tuolumne Visitor Center drive 8.2 miles east on Tioga Road/Highway 120 to the Yosemite Park Tioga Pass entrance. The parking lot is on the left (west) side of the road 100 feet before reaching the exit station.

Hiking directions: From the parking lot, the trail heads west, leading uphill through a lodgepole pine forest. The first 0.6 miles is a steep ascent up a rocky trail to a ridgetop overlooking Middle Gaylor Lake and the majestic peaks that loom in the distance. The trail then descends to the lake. Turn right and closely follow the north shore of Middle Gaylor Lake to the stream inlet. Cross the stream and continue north, to the right, along the west edge of the stream until reaching Upper Gaylor Lake. Stay close to the west shore of Upper Gaylor Lake and continue north. The trail heads up the hillside enroute to the stone cabin and the Great Sierra Mine, which can be seen on the Tioga Hill above. The last 0.2 miles to the buildings is a steep climb. To return, follow the same path back.

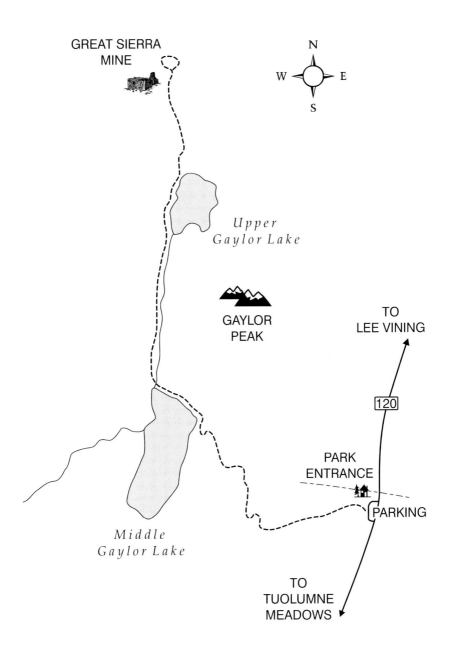

GREAT SIERRA
MINE

N
W E
S

*Upper
Gaylor Lake*

GAYLOR
PEAK

TO
LEE VINING

120

PARK
ENTRANCE

PARKING

*Middle
Gaylor Lake*

TO
TUOLUMNE
MEADOWS

GAYLOR LAKES

Notes

Information Sources

Yosemite National Park
P.O. Box 577
Yosemite National Park, CA 95389
(209) 372-0265

Lodging Reservations
Yosemite Concession Service
5410 E. Home
Fresno, CA 93727
(209) 252-4848

Campground Reservations
Destinet
9450 Carroll Park Drive
San Diego, CA 92121
(800) 436-7275

Wilderness Permits
Yosemite Wilderness Office
P.O. Box 577
Yosemite National Park, CA 95389
(209) 372-0307

High Sierra Camps, reservations
5410 E. Home
Fresno, CA 93727
(209) 454-2002

Yosemite Association
P.O. Box 545
Yosemite National Park, CA 95389
(209) 379-2646

Yosemite Institute
P.O. Box 487
Yosemite National Park, CA 95389
(209) 379-9511

The Yosemite Fund
P.O. Box 637
Yosemite National Park, CA 95389
(415) 434-1782

Road and Weather Information
(209) 372-0200
(900) 454-9673

National Forest District Offices:

Groveland Ranger Station
Stanislaus National Forest
Highway 120 West
(209) 962-7825

Mariposa Ranger Station
Sierra National Forest
Highway 140
(209) 966-3638

Oakhurst Ranger Station
Sierra National Forest
Highway 41
(209) 683-4665

Mono Lake Ranger Station
Inyo National Forest
Highway 120 East
(619) 647-3000

Other Day Hike Guidebooks

___ Day Hikes on Oahu $6.95
___ Day Hikes on Maui 8.95
___ Day Hikes on Kauai 8.95
___ Day Trips on St. Martin 9.95
___ Day Hikes in Denver 6.95
___ Day Hikes in Boulder, Colorado 8.95
___ Day Hikes in Steamboat Springs, Colorado 8.95
___ Day Hikes in Summit County, Colorado 8.95
___ Day Hikes in Aspen, Colorado 7.95
___ Day Hikes in Yosemite National Park
    25 Favorite Hikes 8.95
___ Day Hikes Around Lake Tahoe 8.95
___ Day Hikes in Yellowstone National Park
    25 Favorite Hikes 7.95
___ Day Hikes in the Grand Tetons and Jackson Hole, WY 7.95
___ Day Hikes in Los Angeles
    Malibu to Hollywood 8.95
___ Day Hikes in the Beartooth Mountains
    Red Lodge, Montana to Yellowstone National Park 8.95

These books may be purchased at your local bookstore or they will be glad to order them. For a full list of titles available directly from ICS Books, call toll-free 1-800-541-7323. Visa or Mastercard accepted.

- -

Please include $2.00 per order to cover postage and handling. Please send the books marked above. I enclose $ _____

Name _____

Address _____

City _____ State _____ Zip _____

Credit Card # _____ Exp. _____

Signature _____

1-800-541-7323